ProTeens

colors

identifying the spiritual temperature of your teens

frank hamrick

Colors: Identifying The Spiritual Temperature Of Your Teens

Previously released under the title, *Your Youth Group's Colors Are Showing!: A Summary Look At Five Colors Of Youth Groups*

Frank Hamrick

Copyright © 1995 by Positive Action For Christ, Inc., P.O. Box 1948, 833 Falls Road, Rocky Mount, NC 27802-1948. All rights reserved. No part may be reproduced in any manner without permission in writing from the publisher.

Second Printing 2002

Printed in the United States of America
ISBN: 1-929784-87-2

Designed by Shannon Brown
Edited by Kraig Keck

Published by

table of contents

preface 4
chapter **1** Your Youth Group's Colors Are Showing. 6
       2 Working With An Ice Blue Youth Group 12
       3 Working With A Fresh Green Youth Group 28
       4 Working With A Cool White Youth Group 40
       5 Working With A Warm Yellow Or Fiery Red Youth Group . . 56

preface

For years I've looked for a way to explain to youth pastors and lay youth leaders that there is no one–size–fits–all method to youth work. The average graduate of Bible college comes into his first ministry with tons of great ideas. However, after a few months, or maybe a few years, he is disillusioned because the great ideas that his college gave him haven't worked in his situation. He's even attended the conferences and heard the "experts," but they just don't seem to work in his youth group.

At this point he has to make a decision. He often decides that his teens are just rebels and starts looking for another youth ministry where these ideas will work. Or he may decide that he's a failure in youth ministry and look to get out. However, probably neither of these is true.

A better decision is to analyze his youth group. It may be that the youth pastor has never understood the simple truth that youth groups are different! Teens are different! They are at different levels of spiritual growth and maturity, and that simple fact can spell the difference between the success and failure of a particular method. What the "experts" often fail to mention when touting their particular program is that it took several years for them to develop a youth group where that method would work.

1

your youth group's colors are showing

This book is my attempt to explain this concept using colors to represent different levels of spiritual maturity or progressive sanctification. It is also my attempt to show you how the resources available through ProTeens can meet the needs of these various levels of spiritual growth. Even though you may identify your group in the first few chapters, read the entire book to make sure that you understand the concept completely. My prayer is that this book will encourage you in your youth ministry and give you specific help.

It's youth or consequences,

Frank Hamrick
Rocky Mount, NC

April, 2002

Pete sat at the back of the class. He had rocked back his chair and was leaning against the wall. As Pastor Jeff taught the lesson, Pete and two of his buddies alternated looking out the window and down at the floor; but they seldom looked at Pastor Jeff. Occasionally, when Jeff would give a personal illustration, Pete would look up. If the youth pastor said something funny, several in the class would laugh; but Pete would stare at the others like they were crazy. One of Pete's friends would give a mock laugh, and Pete and the others would snicker. Of course, no one took notes.

Some of the teens closer to the front of the room were politely listening to the lesson. At least they appeared to be listening. But a closer look revealed eyes that were glassy and minds that were preoccupied with other concerns.

Several teens actually had their study books open and would write in the blanks if the youth pastor put something on the overhead. But even that gesture was done halfheartedly and without much thought. Only one or two of the teens were actually involved and interested in what Pastor Jeff was teaching.

Poor Pastor Jeff. Week after week he struggled with a disinterested group of teens. They would come to activities. Most were polite, with the exception of Pete's sullen rebels. But only a couple ever talked to Jeff about spiritual things after class. Those same two teens were memorizing Scripture and doing their devotions in the youth program Pastor Jeff had introduced last fall.

Pastor Jeff continued to challenge the group, but it seemed that nothing was reaching them. He had challenged them to memorize 200 verses of Scripture that year, have daily devotions, take notes at each meeting and take a test on the previous meeting's lesson, read ten Christian books, and go out soul–winning on Saturdays. To get more than a handful to do any of this seemed nearly impossible.

Soon the parents began to complain. "This new youth pastor is simply too boring. He is trying to put the teens through Bible college." "He doesn't have enough fun times. All he ever does is lecture," the pastor was told. Certainly, the new youth program was a bust and needed to be shelved as soon as possible.

What was Pastor Jeff's real problem? Jeff's problem was color matching. He failed to realize the color of his youth group and match his program to that color. Jeff's youth group was ice blue, but Jeff's program was red hot.

Surely you know that all youth groups aren't the same. But did you know that these differences can be expressed in colors? We divide youth groups into the following five color categories.

ice blue

An ice blue youth group is basically an unsaved youth group. The teens have no spiritual concern or depth. They are worldly and totally indifferent to spiritual concerns. (Of course, not every teen will be this way, but this will be the prevalent attitude of an ice blue group.)

An ice blue youth group will respond to an announcement of a hot dog roast with: "It's not the most exciting thing in the world; but, at least it's a good way to meet the chicks, man. Let's go and see if we can't bring life to these Christian types."

fresh green

A fresh green youth group is dominated by new teenagers. They are new either in age (younger teens) or experience (they've never had a youth program, or they are basically new believers). Either way, their main characteristic is enthusiasm. They are unsophisticated and will get excited about almost anything you do.

If you announce to this group that you are having a boring hot dog roast, they will reply: "Fantastic! We've never had anything that exciting around here!"

A youth pastor can't miss with this group. They're ready for anything. They may be unsaved, worldly, young, or new Christians; but they're starved for action. Just announce it, and they will be there.

cool white

This type of youth group is the opposite of the fresh green teens. These kids have seen it all, heard it all, done it all, and are bored with it all. Sadly, they may be Christian school kids. They are sophisticated, spoiled, and cool. Perhaps their parents are upper middle class.

Whether lost or saved (who knows!), they are apathetic. Tell this crowd you're having a hot dog roast, and they will groan, "Boring!"

Nothing moves them. They are truly colorless.

warm yellow

A warm yellow group has some spiritual life. For the most part these teens are actually interested in spiritual things. They will come to Bible study and take notes and maybe even ask questions.

They have a warm family spirit among themselves. They enjoy being together, and they enjoy activities.

Announce a hot dog roast to this youth group, and the general response is: "Well, it's not the coolest thing in the world, but at least it will give us a chance to be together and enjoy each other."

fiery red

This is the spiritually hot youth group. These kids are on fire for the Lord. They not only come to Bible study, but a significant number of them want to serve the Lord with their lives. Many of them go to Christian colleges when they graduate. They witness, they give their testimonies, and they pray fervently. Further, they have a genuine, personal relationship with the Lord.

How does this group respond to a hot dog roast? "Hey, this is a great opportunity to bring my unsaved buddies. Maybe they will get saved."

the colors chart

The Colors Chart on the inside front cover is a graphical representation of the five colors of teens. The order of the colors represents the entire spectrum of spirituality. The fiery red teens are the most spiritually alive (they're your hot core) and the ice blue teens are the most spiritually dead. Notice also that the colors get smaller and smaller as you move to the center. This represents the general truth that the more spiritually hot teens are a smaller percentage of the total youth group than the spiritually dead ones. A teen often moves from unsaved (ice blue), to newly saved and excited (fresh green), to cool–down (cool white), then if growth begins, to warm yellow and red hot.

What color is your youth group? The answer to that question will determine the type of youth program you should have. This book will examine each color and help you reach your group, no matter what its color may be.

2

working with an ice blue youth group

At the bottom of the ladder in spiritual maturity is the ice blue youth group. It is certainly not uncommon. Sad to say, it is far more prevalent than fiery red youth groups.

definition of a blue youth group

What is a blue youth group? Blue is the color your lips and fingers get when they are cold. It describes a group that is characterized by coldness and indifference toward spiritual realities.

Jeff's youth group obviously had a few teens who weren't spiritually blue. But for the most part, we would color his group blue.

a blue youth group is not...

This does not mean, however, that blue teens are unkind, sullen, rebellious, or uncouth. Many in Jeff's group are polite and cooperative. In fact, it was their polite, well-behaved decorum that fooled Jeff. He associated polite behavior with spirituality, only to realize later in the year that these two traits were not necessarily synonymous.

Too often we think of sullen, rebellious teens as unspiritual and place the rest of the group in the spiritual camp. While some ungodly teens have rebellious characteristics, not all do. Many unsaved or unspiritual teens may be model citizens in school, at home, and in church!

A blue youth group may be polite, cooperative, sharp, and well behaved. Many of the teens may be emotionally and socially mature. They may make the best grades in school, know how to treat adults with respect, and may be models of civic and social decorum.

It is often true that the more worldly teens are the most polite and best behaved in school, home, and church. Why is this so? Several reasons may be suggested.

worldly wisdom gives worldly maturity.

It is true that teens who have been around are more worldly–wise. This earthly wisdom is often seen as maturity, which we then consider to be spiritual maturity. Teens who have been raised in a worldly or socially elite environment have learned proper behavior. They have learned that certain behavior pays off in the long run.

Youth who have been sheltered from the world are, in all honesty, simple. This simplicity is often seen as immaturity. Thus, the unsaved are often more mature than the saved. Certainly they have had more exposure to worldly concepts and seem to be with it far more than the more sheltered teens.

This worldly wisdom is often seen as leadership potential by youth pastors and Christian school teachers. The problem is then compounded when the adult leaders place these natural leaders in prominent positions in the church or school. Psalm 12:8 predicts the results: "The wicked walk on every side, when the vilest men are exalted."

"You get what you honor" is a biblical principle. If you thrust these sharp, cool, worldly–wise teens into leadership positions, you will increase their numbers.

We must be careful that we don't mistake politeness, proper manners, courtesy, and citizenship for spiritual maturity.

the spiritually cold may have something to cover up.

Some teens have a reason to be polite. They have a lot to hide! They may get drunk on Saturday night, but they are in church Sunday and are the most polite to the pastor.

Don't be fooled by politeness. It is often feigned because of guilt. It is sometimes a cover-up for a rotten life.

decorum, grades, and cooperation are their goodness.

The world has its own standard of goodness. Look at our civic clubs and organizations. They do a lot of good in our communities, yet many of their members are unsaved. Why? Because helping others, being politically correct, good decorum, and good grades are all part of the world's "religion."

Jeff's group was ice blue, but he didn't realize it until late in the year. Except for Pete and his back-row chair-leaners, most were good kids. Only later did Jeff realize that these good kids had no spiritual appetite.

Don't be fooled by the fact that your teens are polite, kind, helpful, and cooperative. Those qualities, unfortunately, have little parallel with true spiritual life.

a blue youth group is...

A blue youth group is cold spiritually, even though it may be warm socially. There is little interest in Bible study, prayer, daily devotions, or witnessing. The blue youth group simply does not care to study the Word. They may have a curious interest in the Bible (e.g., Where did Cain get his wife? Are airplanes really predicted in the Minor Prophets?), but they have little interest in knowing its greater truths and living them. They may be great on relationships with others, but they know little of a relationship with the Lord.

More than likely, a blue youth group is filled with unsaved teens. They may profess to be saved but may not truly possess salvation. If quizzed, they could give you the correct plan of salvation. They may have made a profession of faith and been baptized. But whether or not God actually saved them is questionable. They show little fruit of salvation.

Blue teens have little desire to attend Bible study; and when they do come, they often don't bring a Bible. They don't care to listen in church or youth group.

Blue teens don't memorize Scripture, don't have devotions, and don't initiate conversations about the Lord.

Further, blue youth groups are worldly-minded. The desire for material things and the desire to sin drive them. (Obviously, we all have a desire to sin, but spiritually mature youth do not constantly give in to this desire.) Many blue teens drink alcoholic beverages on the sly, curse, tell dirty jokes, have low morals (even though some blue teens have high moral standards), and in general have few biblical standards.

If you run a program like ProTeens Classic or Delta Force, the blue youth group will show little enthusiasm. They will not take the quiz, have daily devotions, memorize Scripture, or participate in Practical Christian Work assignments. If they do any of these, it will be the bare minimum and only if their parents force them to get involved.

how to work with a blue youth group

identify them

First, don't make Pastor Jeff's mistake. He failed to identify the color of his youth group before he started his youth program. As a youth pastor, one of your first goals should be to ascertain the color of your youth group. You must match the color of your youth program to the color of your teens; and if you don't know the color of your teens, you are lucky if you happen to get a perfect match.

But how do we identify the color of a youth group? Follow the suggestions below, and your youth group should start showing their colors.

spend time with them

Never start a youth program until you have personally spent quality time with your teens. We are not talking about formal times but informal times. Go with them to ball games, to get a hamburger, to the mall, or to the lake. During these times bring up spiritual topics and watch their responses. Remember, it is not their decorum or manners but their responses to spiritual truth that determine whether or not they are blue.

Many youth pastors make the mistake of mingling with their teens only during youth activities or youth meetings. You will never get to know them that way. You must see them away from church to understand their true colors. More on this later.

take a youth group survey

One of the first things a youth pastor should do when beginning a new ministry is to take a youth group survey. Positive Action For Christ designed a survey that has helped hundreds of youth pastors identify the color of their youth groups.

The key to a good survey is to conceal your purpose for the survey. Teenagers have a way of guessing the answer you want and either throwing you a curve or giving you what you want. We have worded our survey so that the purpose of many of the questions is not as obvious to the teens (even though some of the answers may be obvious).

interview them

Nothing beats a face–to–face meeting with your teens. Obviously, the interviews should be private, since teens are greatly influenced by the presence of their peers. The interview should include many of the questions asked on the survey. However, a good interviewer will add his own questions based on the answers he is receiving. The important element to keep in mind is not necessarily the answers the teens give but the attitudes they display.

You are not looking for correct action but a heart that is warm to spiritual matters. Robots can be taught to give right answers and even imitate right actions; but there is no heart, no feeling, and no warmth of personality to the action taken or the truth given.

Blue teens may know all the biblically correct answers. They may know how to say, "I know I'm saved because the Bible says so." Your questions should center, not so much on knowledge, but on desire. For example, don't ask, "Do you pray?" Instead ask the teen: "What do you get out of prayer? What is the greatest blessing you ever received in prayer?" Rather than asking how a teen knows she is saved, ask her what God has done in her heart that makes her know that God has saved her.

identify with them

Once you have ascertained the color (spiritual temperature) of your teens, you must identify with them. That is, accept them as they are! Be their friend. This is extremely important. Youth pastors generally make two mistakes with ice blue teens.

by avoiding two common mistakes

Unintentional Exclusion

First, youth pastors may unintentionally fail to include ice blue teens in some activities. Since they show little interest in spiritual things, the youth pastor unconsciously fails to include them or show them the same attention and friendliness he gives the more godly teens. This problem is compounded by the guilt or chip on the shoulder many unsaved teens have anyway. Knowing their hearts are not right, they expect to be shunned by godly leaders. They imagine everyone's against them, even when they really aren't. You must make certain that you go out of your way to show such teens that you love them and accept them as they are. You do not like their sin, but you certainly care for their person. This must be clearly evident to these teens.

Negative Motivational Techniques

Second, in a youth pastor's zeal to see his teens at the top of the spiritual thermometer, he may scold and preach down to them. In essence, we mistakenly use negative motivational techniques in an attempt to inspire them to positive living. Rather than encouraging teens to the top, we try to drive them to the top by making them feel guilty. We berate them for their indifference or scold them for their lack of interest. This approach produces guilt but doesn't bring conviction. Decisions based on guilt don't last. In fact, if teens are made to feel guilty often enough, it will lead them to apathy or deeper rebellion.

We must never forget the bottom line with teens—they want to be accepted. If you are to reach them, you must accept them where they are now. A good youth pastor doesn't love teens for what they can be, but he loves them for what they are now. That doesn't mean that we accept their sins, but it does mean that we accept their souls.

Paul emphasizes the words *encouragement* and *edification* in his writings. Teens need to be built up, not torn down. We must demonstrate that we are proud of them. We must enjoy spending time with them. We must let them see that we love them.

Taking the opposite approach to the above mistakes, we identify with our teens in the following two ways.

by mixing and mingling with them

Teens need to know that you care for them, are proud of them, and are on their side. How do they come to this conclusion? By the amount of attention you give them outside of class.

We have already mentioned the importance of taking them to get a hamburger or going shopping with them. Another suggestion is to open your home to them. Your home should be a refuge for teens. They should feel comfortable and wanted at your house, any time of day.

The author made his home a sanctuary for teens. Do you remember Pong? It was the first video game available. My wife and I—

living on a shoestring at the time—bought one of those games, and soon our house was crawling with teens. We kept our refrigerator packed with drinks. Popcorn was a must. Soon our home was the second home of our teens. I put up a basketball goal in the yard to attract the guys. Later I built a Frisbee golf course around our house. We bought all kinds of games. Our furniture was deliberately leisure. We knew there would be spilled drinks, greasy popcorn stains, and broken lamps. That comes with the territory, but there is no better way for teens to know that you really love them.

When they realize that you accept them (you identify with them), they will begin to accept you. They will listen to your preaching and teaching and will start to examine their own lives.

by encouraging them

Paul made much of the words *edify, exhort,* and *comfort.* The Greek words he used mean "to encourage" and "to lift up." While it is true that the truly rebellious need to be warned of the consequences of their sins, the majority of teens aren't rebellious. They simply follow a small nucleus of rebellious leaders. The best way to reach the majority is through positive encouragement.

Scolding, condemning, and chastising may get the attention of the rebellious; but it will only drive the rest away. Schools and churches abound with browbeaten teens who are constantly told that they are ungodly, going to hell, and "the worst kids I've ever taught."

Remember, they probably think negatively of themselves already. You only add to their belief that they aren't worth saving when you condemn them. Be their friend. Show them what they can be in Christ. Believe in what God can do for them and through them. Give them this vision. You will find that some you thought were rebellious were only imitating the rebellious. All they needed was someone to love them, accept them, challenge them, and encourage them.

begin where they are

Blue teens need a blue program, just as infants need milk, babies need baby food, and toddlers need their food cut up. Giving steak to a baby will choke him. In the same way, feeding a fiery red program to blue teens will drive them away. This is why you have to identify their color before you choose your program.

My first night as youth pastor in a new church was an eye opener for me. I planned to begin a verse–by–verse study of Romans. The teens would eat it up, so I thought. Thirty minutes later I was totally dejected. No one listened, except for two girls I saw taking notes. Encouraged, I moved closer to see their notes, only to find that they were doing their homework. Some teens walked out of the class and went home when they thought I had been teaching long enough.

A few weeks of this, and I realized something was wrong. Several activities and surveys later, I realized that I had an ice blue youth group. I readjusted my program accordingly.

Starting with socials and fun times, I got to know the teens. Drawing the teens to my home, I played games, went sledding with them, and played ball with them. I turned our Wednesday night meetings into discussion times. When I spoke to them, I emphasized the evidences of salvation.

Gradually the teens warmed to me and my wife and to my challenges. Over the course of the next year, thirty teens (most of whom were already members of the church) got saved; and the youth group caught fire for the Lord.

The key to this ministry? I abandoned my fiery red program and met the teens at their own spiritual level.

emphasize fun

No matter the color of your youth group, all teens love to have fun. Having fun with teens is a great tool for accomplishing all of the above: (1) it helps you identify them; (2) it helps you identify *with* them, and (3) it meets them where they are.

One of the problems with Christian school teachers is that the teacher doesn't always know how to enjoy his class. Teens need to see that you can laugh, that you are human, that you have a sense of humor, and that you can take a joke.

Some have the philosophy that you should not get too close to your students, or they will lose respect for you. Nonsense! The closer you get to your teens—if you are what you ought to be—the more they should admire you and want to be like you.

Fun times can break down barriers that keep teens from listening to your messages or following your leadership.

Our living room has been the scene of basketball tournaments and even tackle football! We had teens coming out of our ears. Blue kids, along with the green, white, yellow, and red kids all came to our home. Why? We made it a fun place to be.

emphasize the evidences of salvation and the gospel message

Unsaved teens need two types of gospel messages: get lost messages and get saved messages. Most of us preach get saved messages but know little about how to preach get lost messages.

Get saved messages are great for those who are lost and know they are lost. But these messages have little impact on those who are lost but think they are saved.

Telling a lost teen about the horrors of hell will not affect him if he thinks he is saved. He has to get lost before he will be concerned about getting saved.

How do we get a teen lost who mistakenly thinks he is saved? By preaching get lost messages. These are sermons designed to show the infallible evidences of salvation. Some evidences are fallible. That is, they may be faked, but other evidences are infallible. For example, going to church is not an evidence of salvation. Reading the Bible is not an evidence. Witnessing is not even an evidence! However, a hunger to know the Word, a longing to pray, and a desire to obey God's Word are evidences that one is saved.

Ice blue teens often think they are saved. They must be confronted with their lost condition by the preaching of the evidences of salvation.

how ProTeens can help you reach your ice blue youth group

Positive Action For Christ has designed a number of tools to help a youth pastor identify and reach an ice blue youth group. Consult the Positive Action For Christ Youth Ministry catalog or our web site for further descriptions of these and other products.

recreation

Our Recreation books (four volumes are available) contain hundreds of recreational ideas to help you have fun with your youth group while getting to know them and identifying with them. These games, activities, and events are proven winners. They have been used by hundreds of youth groups around the world for 25 years.

hot shots

Hot Shots are a series of Bible lessons designed by Positive Action For Christ for entry level teens. They deal with hot topics of teen concern and emphasize group participation. Rather than lecture, these lessons use group dynamics such as role–playing, discussion, visual aids, debate, and object lessons to drive their truths home to teens.

Each study is five lessons long (enough lessons for one month, although some youth leaders spend two weeks per lesson) and includes pages you may copy and hand out in class. Thus, your teens do not have to purchase a separate student's book. Check our catalog or web site for currently available Hot Shot topics.

milk: for new christians

Positive Action For Christ publishes a Christian Growth Series of small self–study books. Each book is eight chapters long and deals with the basic beliefs of the Christian life. A teacher's guide is available for those who would like to teach these books in a class setting. (For more information, see our web site.)

The first book in this series is *Milk*. This book is designed for the unsaved or the newly saved. It has been used with fourth graders through senior citizens. It has been studied in discipleship classes, onboard ships in the Mediterranean, by new believers in the Gulf War, in Sunday school classes, and on many mission fields. It has been translated into many languages and can be found all over the world.

Milk deals with the basics: how to get saved, the assurance of salvation, how to study the Bible, how to pray, how to witness, baptism, the local church, and tithing. One book is needed per student. The teacher's guide contains discussion questions and extra material to help guide your students through the book. It is ideal for the ice blue youth group.

teen survey sheets

Special color matching survey sheets are available from Positive Action For Christ. See our web site for details.

ProTeens sigma youth program

Sigma is a youth program designed specifically for entry level youth groups (blue, green, and white). If you find that your youth group is ice blue, Sigma is a program you should seriously consider. For a further description of this program, see www.positiveaction.org.

ProTeens classic blue youth program

ProTeens Classic is the name of our tried and true ProTeen club that has been around for over thirty years. Thousands of churches and tens of thousands of teens have been challenged and reached through this program. In 1996, we started making color versions of ProTeens Classic. The blue version is designed precisely for those youth groups that are predominantly blue in color.

Do you need to charter with ProTeens to purchase any of the above? You must charter only if you use one of our three youth club programs (Sigma, Classic, or Delta Force). All of the other materials may be purchased by anyone, whether chartered or not.

One final question lingers. What's the difference between Sigma and Classic Blue? Classic is a much more involved program. It is an all–encompassing program that includes Scripture memory, daily devotions, Christian outreach, reading Christian books, a 30–week Bible study, and weekly written quizzes. While originally designed for the committed, mature spiritual teen, it is now available in different levels of difficulty. While the weekly lesson doesn't change, the demands do vary. For example, a blue youth group would memorize 30 verses a year while a red youth group would memorize 180 verses a year. Thus, as your teens progress, you can change the demands and challenge of your program without having to change programs. Some of your teens can be on Classic Blue while others are on Classic Red.

Sigma, on the other hand, is an evangelistic program aimed squarely at meeting the needs of teens at the entry level while offering outreach opportunities for teens of all spiritual colors and temperatures.

3

working with a fresh green youth group

"I've never had it so good as a youth pastor," Pastor Bob told fellow Pastor Jeff. "These teens get excited about anything I do. I can't make a mistake!"

Pastor Jeff couldn't believe his ears. "Boy, I wish my teens were like that," he replied. "I could rent out the Taj Mahal for an overnight activity, and they wouldn't get excited! You must have a godly youth group," Jeff wondered aloud.

Bob wrinkled his forehead as he thought about that. He didn't even know if some of his kids were saved, much less godly. Yet their enthusiasm was undeniable.

Why are these youth groups so different? Is one group saved and the other lost? Actually, Jeff and Bob pastor two different colors of youth groups. Jeff's group is ice blue, and Bob's group is fresh green.

The fresh green youth group is one step up the ladder from the ice blue youth group. These teens may or may not be saved. They may or may not be spiritual. The one common denominator of a fresh green youth group is unsophisticated enthusiasm.

definition of a green youth group

Green is the color of new life and growth. Thus, it describes a group that exhibits the joy of excitement and enthusiasm. There's a springtime freshness in this group.

This is typical of a youth group that (1) is dominated by younger teens, (2) is dominated by newly saved teens and/or (3) has never had a lively youth program before.

Youth pastors fortunate enough to be in such a situation find that they can do nothing wrong…for six months! Everything they do is new, exciting, and welcomed. A hot dog roast is an extravaganza!

a green youth group is not…

A word of warning, however. Excitement is not the same as spiritual life. The greening of the youth group may not last. Jesus warns of those plants that spring up quickly and just as soon fade away. Therefore, a green youth group is not …

necessarily a saved youth group

Youthful exuberance may be grounded in the age of the teens. Junior high teens are generally more gung ho for activities than older teens. Anything you do sounds exciting.

Youthful exuberance may also be grounded in the newness of the youth program. We all get excited about something new. The real test of the teen's spiritual life is six months later—are they still excited about Bible study? Many teens start the ProTeen year with lots of excitement, only to drop out a few months or weeks later when the newness is gone.

Remember Christ's words in Matthew 13:20–21. Here He warns of the one who receives the word "with joy" (enthusiasm or excitement) but because he has no "root in himself" only endures "for a while." Why? Because "when tribulation or persecution ariseth because of the word, by and by he is offended." This is the unsaved fresh green youth group.

This is not to suggest that all enthusiastic gung ho groups are lost. But it is a warning that a youth group's enthusiasm is not to be mistaken for spiritual life.

Furthermore, a green youth group, with all of its excitement, friendliness, and freshness, is not ...

necessarily a growing youth group

A second mistake in color identity is to think that an excited, responding youth group is a spiritually growing youth group. If there is no life there, the growth will not last. In the same Parable of the Sower in Matthew 13, Christ reminds us that the "stony ground" hearer endures "for a while." There is a time when he seems to be growing. But trials and the test of time prove that he has no "root in himself." That is, he was not saved from the beginning, even though he showed signs that just maybe he had been transformed.

A green youth group will endure for a while; but if they aren't saved, they will not make it past the newness stage. September finds them excited, but January finds them wilted.

Again, keep in mind, some green youth groups are truly saved; and in those cases the freshness, excitement, and growth will continue throughout the year. (Of course, every teen will have his good and bad times; but generally speaking, the group will keep on course.)

a green youth group is...

ready to try something new

Bored by the fact that they have never really had a youth leader and/or a youth program or excited because they just got saved or gung ho because they are junior highers getting their first taste of a youth ministry, we can say one thing for sure: a green youth group is ready for something new! Anything you suggest they are ready to try.

one that runs on its emotions

Green teens receive the Word "with joy." They are emotional. Most younger teens are far more exuberant and emotional (at least on the outside) than older teens. Thus, green youth do what they feel like doing. They don't have the maturity or character to do what is right just because it is right. Their feelings control them.

unpredictable

A green youth group is like a hurricane. You never know where it will go next. You will be uncertain whether their enthusiasm comes from true spiritual life or whether it is the result of more worldly reasons. Girls may be excited about a youth program because a lot of good–looking guys are attending (or vice versa). So enjoy the fun while it lasts, youth pastor! Six months from now, the handsome guy moves away and some of the girls will quit coming.

Character and maturity produce stability. Since a green teen runs on his emotions, you will not see as much stability and faithfulness in his participation, attention span, and interest level. One week he is hot; the next he is cold.

how to work with a green youth group

Having described the green youth group, let's discuss the methods that work best with them. We are assuming that you have already taken the steps discussed in the blue youth group chapter (that is, you have given the survey, interviewed them, and identified with them) and have determined that they are fresh green.

What are your next steps?

take advantage of their enthusiasm

A wise youth pastor will take advantage of the youthful unsophisticated enthusiasm of his group. "Make hay while it is day" applies to the green youth group.

have fun with them

Sophisticated, spoiled teens are bored with anything you do—but not fresh green teens. They will howl at even your corniest jokes. Take advantage of this time in your youth group experience.

Our youth group's first activities included a GOO (a Christian version of a Grand Ole Opry) and a GOO, TWO (two years later, another GOO). Our church people and our teens had never seen anything like this, and we had over 300 people come to the activities.

During those early years, I played some of my craziest games with the teens. We just had down-home, unsophisticated fun. We played Barefooted Marble Pickup, and the teens loved it. I could never get by with that years later!

Enjoy your teens. Enjoy their enthusiasm. You need to be enthusiastic yourself if you are to lead them.

attempt simple studies first

Begin with simple studies like our *Milk* or *Meat*. You do not want to kill their enthusiasm by giving them a heavier diet than they are capable of digesting. However, give them something of substance during the fresh green experience. Their enthusiasm will allow you to begin a simple Bible study with them. Here you will see whether they are truly saved or lost. Even with a simple Bible study, the unsaved green teens will soon lose their enthusiasm. But this is still the best time to start a Bible study. If your teens are green, you can start a Bible study class; and enthusiasm will carry it, at least initially.

move gradually to more difficult studies

This step is taken only if you have a nucleus of teens who are devouring the simple studies and are ready for more. Be careful, however, that you are not appealing to a few at the expense of the majority. You are trying to bring the entire youth group (obviously, you won't get them all) along with you as you move the teens towards the core of the Colors Chart.

introduce a simple scripture memory program

Teens must hide God's Word in their hearts if they are to grow and have victory over sin. Thus, they must be led to memorize Scripture. However, like anything else, let them memorize in moderation. Don't strangle them with too great a challenge. Green grass can take rough traffic after it has matured and taken root, but until that time it can be crushed by too much use. So green teens need time to mature. Give them a few verses to memorize at the beginning and give them the taste of accomplishment. Then, give them a greater challenge.

In my first ProTeen program, I required the group to memorize 75 verses of Scripture the first year. The teens were overwhelmed. Most didn't even try. (I had to lower the standard before the year was over.) However, two teens did respond and memorized all 75 verses. The next year the total was raised to 90. Again, those same two teens memorized 90 verses. But the exciting statistic was that nearly half of the group memorized 75 verses! The following year I increased the demands again. This continued over the years until

I had teens memorizing all 360 verses of Scripture for the year in one week!

Remember, however, this took ten years to achieve. If I had started by challenging my fresh green group to memorize 360 verses, none of them would have tried and they would all have felt like failures. The next year no one would have joined the youth group. Set a standard the teens can realistically achieve and award the teens for their progress.

add a devotional program to your expanding youth ministry

If your teens are fresh green, they may not be ready for devotions their first year. Again, give them something simple and watch the results. Remember, you want to encourage your teens, not discourage them. Give them something you will be able to award. If no one will meet up to your devotional standard, then you will only make them feel guilty and will probably fuss at them over it until they feel worthless and quit doing anything for the Lord.

However, if several of your teens respond, keep it up and encourage other teens to try it. Positive Action For Christ has several devotional plans available for fresh green teens.

award them for their achievements

Encourage your teens' accomplishments with nice, meaningful awards. Many award banquets are almost a disgrace. I've seen churches have a sports banquet one week followed by a ProTeen Awards Banquet the following week. The comparison was astonishing. The sports banquet was an extravagant event. Expensive trophies were given to cool jocks who had no spiritual life. Scores of proud, gloating adults gave standing ovations and slaps on the back to the winners. Large steaks were served, and a famous athlete gave the address. The following week a ProTeen Awards Banquet was held after church in a Sunday school department. A few parents attended; and the Scripture memory, quiz, and total scoring champions were given small plastic "gold" cups while everyone politely applauded.

No wonder we don't produce godly youth! Remember, you get what you honor. If you honor athleticism, you will get it. If you honor cool kids, you will get them. If you honor godly teens, you will reap godly teens. Psalm 12:8 warns, "The wicked walk on every side, when the vilest men are exalted."

Make your awards program special. Spend the last dollar of your youth budget on it if you must. We must show teens that godliness is important to us and to them. A cheap award will make them think that what they did to earn it was cheap.

Nothing is more important than Scripture memory and Bible study. Prove it to your teens with your awards!

By the way, make your awards spiritually significant. One youth leader gave away a CD player to the teen who brought the most visitors to Sunday school. Later he realized that the teen was using it to play the world's music. Don't feed a teen's greed with your awards. Rather, feed his soul. A week at a great Christian camp, a Christian college scholarship, a scholarship toward the next missions trip, an expensive Bible or commentary, and free ProTeen materials the following year are a few possibilities for awards that encourage spiritual progress.

Recognition by the pastor in the Sunday morning worship service is another must. The pastor must show his serious approval of what these teens have accomplished.

expose them to christian colleges, camps, and other solid youth groups

Fresh green teens may have no idea that there are other teens doing what they are doing. They have a great need to belong. When they find out that other youth groups are doing what they are doing, it excites them and fires their enthusiasm to greater heights.

A trip to a sound Christian college will expose them to young people who are serious about the Lord. Exposure to a great Christian camp will let them see other youth groups with exciting programs.

The author recalls an incident at one of the first ProTeen weeks at The Wilds Camp in Rosman, North Carolina. A young lady stopped him to say: "Mr. Hamrick, I'm coming back next year and will be one of the top scorers in the nation! I was the top scorer in our youth group with 1,500 points. I thought I had really done something until I came to The Wilds. I heard teens talking about 4,000 and 5,000 points and perfect scores on their quizzes. I couldn't believe it. I didn't think any Christian teen did things like that! Now I see what I can do. Look out for me next year!"

how ProTeens can help reach your fresh green youth group

blue Positive Action For Christ materials

Many of the materials used with a blue youth group are just as effective with a green group (e.g., *Milk*, Recreation, and Hot Shots). Why? Because the green group may be just as lost as the blue group! The only difference is the greater enthusiasm and unspoiled, unsophisticated excitement of the green teens. Review the chapter on blue teens to see if there are Positive Action For Christ materials mentioned there that would be useful with your green group.

meat: for growing christians

In addition to the blue materials, *Meat* is an ideal study book for your green youth group. This book is the second in our Christian Growth Series. *Meat* consists of eight chapters on the major doctrines of the Word. It is written in a simple manner so as to appeal to entry level Christians. *Meat* is a perfect follow–up to *Milk*.

ProTeens sigma youth program

Even though the Sigma program was suggested for the blue group, it is just as ideal for the green group. The enthusiasm of the green group will make the society competition take off. In fact, ProTeens Sigma will probably work better with a green group than with a blue group.

ProTeens classic green youth program

As mentioned in the chapter on blue teens, ProTeens Classic now comes in four different colors. The green version requires more Scripture memory verses, more books, and more quizzes than the blue version, but not so much as to choke or discourage your teens. Their enthusiasm will create great individual scoring competition. If you have teens that respond to a challenge, ProTeens Classic Green should be given serious consideration.

Remember, Sigma and Classic are complete programs, not just curriculum. For more information, see www.positiveaction.org

ancient landmarks

Ancient Landmarks is the ideal book for teens who know little about personal standards of separation. It teaches teens to establish their own personal standards based on thirteen biblical principles and to set them as immovable "ancient landmarks" in their lives. Their standards are recorded in their *Ancient Landmarks* journal for future reference. Ten years later they can look back and see whether or not they have drifted from their moorings or whether they are still anchored to their ancient landmarks.

five smooth stones

Developed by Rand Hummel of The Wilds, *Five Smooth Stones* is a Scripture memory program that can double as a devotional book for beginning Christian youth. Each volume contains 15–18 chapters of verses. Each chapter contains five verses (smooth stones) to defeat a "giant" in our lives (such as pride, laziness, worldliness, materialism, TV, rock music, or greed). A review is built into the program to keep the verses fresh in teens' minds.

4

working with a cool white youth group

Pastor Bob was excited about the great turnout he had for his latest activity—a fish fry. Pastor Lee was incredulous. *How could Bob get teens excited about a fish fry?* he wondered. *I couldn't get my teens excited if I gave away pizzas!* Lee's kids yawned during the lesson. They looked at their watches. They looked out the window. Yet they were mostly Christian school kids. They could tell you all about the Rapture of the Church and knew the books of the Bible backwards and forwards. Bob's kids hardly knew the Bible. But what enthusiasm they had!

"If I were to describe my teens as a color, " Bob said, "they would be bright green! They're full of energy and life."

Lee thought for a moment. "I'd paint mine white," Lee replied. "They're colorless. They have it all in their heads, but they don't have any energy or excitement."

Lee and Bob realized that they had opposite colors of youth groups. Bob had a fresh green group, and Lee had a cool white group.

Technically, white is not a color. It is the absence of color. As such, white speaks of death. It speaks of coolness. It speaks of blandness. The white of an egg is tasteless.

definition of a white youth group

The white youth group is the cool youth group. All of the above words and a few more describe them: colorless, cool, bland, tasteless, washed-out, and faded. Try to preach to this group, and even the preacher goes to sleep!

The cool white youth group is sophisticated, spoiled, and callused. It has seen it all, heard it all, done it all, and is bored with it all. This youth group is the opposite of the fresh green teens.

In many ways, the white youth group is lower on the color scale than the green youth group—the only difference being that the white may be truly saved without enthusiasm while the green may be lost with enthusiasm.

Sad to say, many Christian school teens fall into the cool white category. They have had chapel five days a week in addition to Wednesday and Sunday church services and Sunday school. They have been preached to nearly nine times a week for twelve years!

They have been told what to do and what not to do. They have been forced into a mold by school–imposed rules. (We aren't saying that rules are unnecessary; we're only showing the downside of an overemphasis on the externals.) Gradually, they have adopted the Christian lifestyle, look, and language. Yet their hearts may be as black as midnight! Their attitudes may be full of envy, greed, and bitterness. One word says it all about this group—apathy.

a white youth group is not...

excited

Forget generating excitement in this crowd. The more you act excited, the more certain they are not to smile or get excited. After all, excitement is uncool.

Jokes usually don't go over with a cool white youth group. The youth pastor thinks they are laughing with him when they are really laughing at him.

cool

Interestingly, cool white teens are not really cool. I often tell teens that really cool people don't have to act like it! If I have to act like I'm cool, I'm not—I'm only acting.

Truly cool people don't have to impress anyone. They don't try to act sullen or mask their emotions. Cool people laugh, they cry, and they want to do what's right. Feigning coolness is immaturity. It's proof that you aren't cool at all. The guys that refuse to laugh when the rest of the youth group laughs at something funny or the guy that rolls his eyes and looks at his cool buddy with a swagger when the speaker tells a joke is really not cool. He is pretending. He is aching for attention.

unreachable

Cool whites are reachable! Some of the greatest Christian leaders were once cool whites. Most cool whites are crying for help. They do have emotions. They cry silently, but they do cry.

The right approach will break the stony heart and melt the hard-set face. Cool whites can become white hot for the Lord!

necessarily unsaved

Cool whites are not necessarily unsaved. Many of them are simply browbeaten Christians or immature teens looking for acceptance. Don't write them off. They may be the source of your greatest joy as the warmth of your approach melts the facade of their appearance.

a white youth group is...

spoiled

Most cool white youth groups have seen it all and done it all. They may come from upper middle class families. A number of them wear expensive designer-label clothes, drive better cars than the youth pastor, and take their dad's boat to the lake on the weekends.

Other cool whites have been exposed to all types of games and activities by previous youth pastors or youth programs. You could never top what's already been done.

What once was exciting to this group is now old hat. Announce a basketball activity to this crowd and see them yawn.

usually browbeaten

If told you are no good or unspiritual long enough, you choose to believe it and act accordingly. Many youth leaders make the tragic mistake of browbeating teens with a Bible. Teens are told how ungodly their clothes are, how wicked their mischief is, and how stupid they are to love the world. Yet all of these things are normal with teens!

It is not ungodly for a teen to want to look like his peers, no matter what their style. It is not wicked for a teen to be mischievous. (Obviously, some things that pass as mischief are wicked.) It is not stupidity that leads a teen to love the world (even though love for the world is folly). We all love the world if we are honest! It is our old nature that craves the world.

It is sad that in our zeal to see Christian teens lead godly lives, we attack normal desires and make them ungodly. There is a better way.

Once more, let's qualify what we are saying. We are not saying that teens should be allowed to sin and practice wickedness. But we are saying that a lot of things we denounce in teens are simply the results of their lack of maturity or experience.

Further, we are not saying that we should not preach against sin. We must preach against sin, but a lot of what we call sin is not sin at all. Sometimes it is merely youth. For example, Christian school leaders sometimes load children down with demerits or punishment for forgetting a pencil. Children are supposed to forget pencils! Should we punish them for being children?

Teens need to be allowed to be teens. That means they will make immature decisions; or due to lack of experience, they will botch a responsibility. This doesn't mean they are ungodly. It only means that they are teenagers. Rather than preaching down to them, we need to show them a better way.

Realize that some things we call sin are not caused by sin at all but by a lack of experience or immaturity. Categorizing their every mistake as sin breeds frustration in teens' hearts and leads to bitterness and dismay. They see no hope for themselves. They are not told that these things are due to their immaturity and youth. They are simply led to believe that they are ungodly. The danger is they may give up on the Christian life long before they are mature enough to live the Christian life.

We are expecting adult conformity from non–adults. Teens are neither adults nor children. They are in between. One day they act responsibly, and the next they revert to being a child. This oscillation leads them to make foolish mistakes. It is vital that we realize this and not be so swift to condemn them.

Browbeaten youth groups will not listen to a preacher—especially if he speaks about standards. They have been spoken to so unkindly and so piously for so long that they are bitter, apathetic, and have long since given up.

While we must preach against sin, we must not condemn our youth to hell for every failure to conform to our standards and rules.

working with a cool white youth group

wanting attention, acceptance, unconditional love, and understanding

Most teens want nothing more than acceptance. They see condemnatory preaching as a rejection of their person. They hear our sermons as saying to them: "If you do what I say, I will like you. Otherwise, I'm not interested in you."

Sometimes, all it takes is a smile, a friendly touch or a conversation about something of importance to a teen to warm his heart to your person. Yet we are so vindictive, so adamant, and so unbending in our rules and regulations that the teen sees nothing attractive in our lives.

Paul had little mercy for a young man by the name of John who had failed as a teenager (Acts 15:37–38). Barnabas (whose name means encourager) was of a different mind. Barnabas believed that John's failure was not sin but was simply his youthfulness. Who was right? History proves that Barnabas probably saved John's spiritual life. He is the same John Mark who later wrote the second book of the New Testament. Later Paul admitted that he had need of this same John Mark (2 Timothy 4:11).

usually led by a few

Cool whites are usually led by a few truly rebellious teens. The followers (the great majority) are really not rebellious nor cool. They are simply trying to find acceptance. They have learned that a certain body language, a certain dress, and a certain lifestyle will bring that acceptance. Craving attention and acceptance, they conform to that lifestyle. Yet if you were to see inside the heart of most of the cool whites, you would find a heart that really wants to do right.

dying for reality

Cool whites have seen so much hypocrisy (at least they think it is hypocrisy), that they are turned off by most preachers, schoolteachers, and Christian leaders. Embittered by being browbeaten while seeing goody-goodies being pushed to the front by these same browbeaters has turned them off to Christianity. They know that many of the goody-goodies are actually fakes who have the youth leader fooled. The rest of the youth group sits back and thinks the whole scene is a farce.

What do cool whites want? They want to see a genuine Christian who loves them for who they really are. They are looking for reality in someone's life, not just loud preaching or browbeating. They are looking for someone who has a genuine relationship with the Lord. They long to know if there is really anything to devotions and prayer. They have seen the ritual; now they want to see the reality in someone's life.

how to work with a white youth group

don't try to dazzle them

First, don't try to dazzle them with the coolest youth activity in the world. They've already seen it. They don't need more razzle-dazzle; they want reality.

Don't get caught up in the bigger-and-better cycle. You're not in competition with the previous youth pastor or the youth program down the road. You're not even in competition with your own self.

Keep your activities simple (with an occasional extravaganza), and you remove a lot of pressure from yourself and the group. Remember, you are going to show them reality, not fluff.

listen to them

give them your time

Teens want your time more than your advice. They may need your advice, but they don't know it. Only as you give them your time will they take your advice.

let them talk

When teens talk, listen! Stop what you're doing and listen. If you're teaching a lesson and one of them asks a question, listen. Answer it, and ask for more questions. Sometimes you accomplish more in an informal, unplanned discussion than in a prepared lesson.

let them know you understand them

Don't ever condemn them for what they say, even if it is wrong. Never embarrass them publicly. Do your very best to understand their argument, even if it's against your point. Try to see where they're coming from and say as much. If they don't sense that you understand them, they will clam up. *Why talk? He doesn't even try to understand what I'm saying!* they think.

create a safe environment for guts talking

Teens need a safe environment where they can spill their guts. They are afraid to tell how they really think because of the reactions of adults. They can't talk to Mom and Dad because they go into a tirade. They can't tell the teachers because they would give them demerits. So they just keep it in.

What is a safe environment? It is one where the leader will not be shocked (at least outwardly) at what the teen has to say. It is one where the leader won't condemn the teen for his thoughts, weird as they may be. It is one in which the leader will be just as accepting and loving of the teen after he has spilled his guts as before. It is one where he knows the leader will not run straight to his parents or break his confidentiality.

lead them; don't drive them

Teens need leaders, not cattle drivers. They want to see someone come in and show them by example. Cool whites are more impressed by action than words. They are reached by a leader who has his devotions faithfully, who witnesses enthusiastically, and who prays with depth and fervor. They are not impressed with someone who merely preaches about those dynamics.

find the ringleaders and isolate their followers

Generally, a few lead the many. This principle is true in all of society. Communism was nothing more than a few elitists controlling the masses. In the Apostle John's day, there was Diotrephes who tried to run the church (3 John 9). In the modern church there are generally a few who control the attitudes of the church. So it is in youth groups. Most teens aren't rebellious; they only act like the two or three rebellious teens who influence them the most.

First Thessalonians 5:14 mentions three types of problem church members. These three types are found in every youth group as well. They are the unruly, the feebleminded, and the weak. A study of the Greek words behind each of these English words gives a clear picture of most problem youth (those who are either blue or white).

Unruly means rebellious. These are the ringleaders. They don't love the Lord and don't care that they don't. They have made their choices against God and have no intention of even pretending to love Him.

Feebleminded literally means "small souled." It can be translated "faint–hearted." In essence, it means easily discouraged. This is the person who gives up when he fails. This person may have a desire to live for the Lord but can't handle failure. He is so easily discouraged that at the first criticism or the first failure on his part, he throws in the towel and says: "That's it. I quit! I can't live the Christian life. Why try?"

Weak translates a word that means "without strength." This is the teen with little character. He doesn't have a strong will. He is a Christian chameleon. His actions are determined by the people he is with at the moment. Again, he may want to live for the Lord, but he doesn't have the character to do so.

You will note that only one of these three types is truly rebellious—the unruly. You will also note that each must be treated differently. The unruly must be warned. The feebleminded (easily discouraged) must be comforted. The weak must be supported.

Rebellious teens understand only one thing—strong warnings. Not denunciations of their character but warnings about the future results of their actions.

The easily discouraged, however, must be comforted. That is, they must be encouraged. Strong words will discourage them further. To call an easily discouraged teen an ungodly teen is to condemn him to further discouragement. Many unthinking youth leaders, schoolteachers, and well-meaning parents have made the sad mistake of treating the easily discouraged the same as the unruly. This will devastate the easily discouraged. He needs encouragement.

The difficulty lies in discerning between the truly rebellious teen and the easily discouraged teen. They often act exactly alike! Both sit in the back of the class and pay little attention to the lesson. Neither does their devotions, takes the quiz, or memorizes Scripture. Yet they are not the same. They need to be treated differently. One needs warning, and the other needs comfort. The one group (the rebellious who are generally in the smaller group) doesn't have any desire to live for God. The other does. One is truly rebellious, and the other is only imitating the rebellious. They tried living for the Lord; but because of failure, they gave up. Thus, they assume that they are ungodly, no good, and are "bound for the pit of hell." At least that's what everyone says about them.

How do you know the difference? Through personal contact and counseling you will see a single difference between the truly rebellious teens and the easily discouraged teens. The easily discouraged will confide in you that they want to live for the Lord and that they have tried to live for the Lord, but it just didn't seem to work for them. So they quit. You will never get this admission from the rebellious, however. They don't mind telling you that they want no part of Christianity.

Further, the weak (the third group) will admit the same as the easily discouraged. A young man once told the author: "I wish I could stay at camp all year. Then I could live for the Lord. But the minute I get home, I know what will happen. That old crowd will come around, and before long I'll be doing the same things they do." That's the confession, not of a rebel, but of a weak teen. He needs support. That is, he needs the physical presence of stronger teens and adult leaders who will spend time with him and be his crutch until he is strong enough to stand on his own.

The point is that the weak and the easily discouraged make up the majority of your problem youth. The rebellious make up a tiny minority yet wield a huge influence.

A good illustration of a youth group is seen in space science. The earth represents a small nucleus of energy. Around it revolves hundreds of satellites sent up by NASA. These satellites revolve around the earth until they are sucked in by its gravitational pull. When we send someone to the moon, we must make a rocket powerful enough to blast out of the gravitational pull of the earth. At last, the gravity of the moon takes over and pulls the spaceship to its orbit.

This shows us how we can reach the easily discouraged and the weak. We must get them out from under the influence of the ungodly and under the influence of the godly.

How do we accomplish this? One way to do this is to have prayer meetings in your home. The rebellious will not be interested in coming. Generally, only the spiritually hot teens will come. Each week, pick out one or two weak or easily discouraged teens and give them a special invitation to come (although everyone is always invited so that those who come do not develop an elitist mentality). In this way you get them away from the ungodly influence and under the influence of the godly. Gradually, they will begin to grow. After a while, pick out another "satellite" teen and get him to come to the prayer meeting.

Whatever you do, you must weaken the influence of the few rebellious teens in your group and enhance the influence of the godly.

honor the hot teens

Here's one of the key points in developing a nucleus of hot teens. Remember our principle from Psalm 12:8—you get what you honor. That holds true here.

Never make a cool, ungodly teen a leader in your group. He doesn't make announcements, he isn't called on to pray, and he is never made captain of a team.

Even if your hot teens are nerds, put them in leadership positions. Remember, you get what you honor. Honor those who really try to live for the Lord. You do this with super banquets, nice (not cheap) awards, public recognition, and giving them the leadership positions in your youth group.

"But what if I don't have any hot teens?" you ask. Then let adults lead until such time as you see certain teens responding. Then give those teens the lead.

be genuine

Don't try to out-cool the cool whites. Being cool isn't what it's all about in Christian work anyway. We are to be on fire for the Lord, not cool for the Lord! If you try to be cool, your teens will be quick to see it. Teens despise adults who try to act like a teenager.

Teens hate hypocrisy. They want reality. Be yourself. Be genuine. Don't put on an act. They will appreciate your honesty and the fact that you are real.

get them involved in church

We have saved the most important tip for reaching the cool whites until last. One word summarizes how to affect the lives of the cool white—service, service, service!

One of the chief reasons teens are cool white is because they have taken in all their lives but have had little opportunity for giving out. They are like the Dead Sea which takes in two billion gallons of water a day yet has no outlet, except for evaporation.

Nothing will kill a youth group faster than (1) taking in more than they give out or (2) giving out more than they are taking in. These must be balanced. Most church youth have Sunday school, Christian school, and ProTeens (or another youth program). Seven days a week they take in Scripture. Yet they don't even know any unsaved teens! They never have to take a stand; they never have to face true persecution; they never hear God's Word attacked or denounced.

Living in a sanitized environment, they develop little immunity to disease. They actually become weaker than teens who take in but get out into the world (either in a job, in public schools, or in faithful witnessing).

One of the most important tools of a youth pastor is to get his teens—especially if they are cool whites—into Christian service.

how ProTeens can help reach your cool white youth group

blue and green materials

As before, the blue and green Positive Action For Christ youth materials will also help the cool white.

ProTeens sigma program

ProTeens Sigma has a special service emphasis with dozens of ideas that get your Sigma societies involved in ministering. In fact, one of the chief ideas behind ProTeens Sigma is ministry. Many youth pastors testify to this part of Sigma waking their youth group up and literally transforming a dead youth group into a group that is on fire for the Lord.

ProTeens classic white youth program

The white version of ProTeens Classic gives more points for Christian service than for anything else. The white group is knowledge rich but output poor, thus the extra emphasis on ministry with ProTeens Classic White.

the boredom cycle

We suggest that every youth group study this important book. It was written for the cool white teen who finds himself bored with life. It shows him why he is bored and how to break out of the boredom cycle and live an exciting, joy–filled Christian life. Your teens may read it, or you may take a couple of weeks to teach it to them.

mighty through God

This Delta Force study is especially helpful to the teen that goes through the motions but has no true devotion in his life. It can literally transform a youth group. Its focus is on teaching teens to meditate in the Word of God so that they see how wonderful He truly is.

5

working with a warm yellow or fiery red youth group

"I praise the Lord for Marathon Day," Jan testified, "because it's the first time this year that our whole youth group has been together! We're family, and it's good to get us all here." Pastor Frank was listening intently to the testimonies of his youth group at the close of his first Marathon Day activity. The teens had been divided into junior high and senior high groups since September. It was now mid-January, and he had a united activity with the entire youth group together.

Jan's testimony surprised him. Jan was a senior high girl, but she was glad to be with seventh graders! Other teens joined in to confirm Jan's opinion. *Boy,* Frank thought, *these teens really want to be together. I didn't realize they were unhappy with splitting up the group.* The testimony service must have lasted a half-hour, and in the process one teen accepted Christ as his Lord and Savior!

What Frank didn't know at the time was that he had a warm yellow youth group. Within the next four years he would see them become a fiery red group. Most of the fiery red group went to Bible College, built their own library of Bible commentaries, learned and practiced the art of scriptural meditation, and won many souls to the Lord. From this group came preachers, missionaries, and youth pastors who today are serving the Lord around the world.

Welcome to the world of warm yellow and fiery red youth groups! Since the warm yellow and fiery red youth groups are similar, we will deal with both of them together.

definition of the yellow and red youth groups

the warm yellow youth group

A yellow group is known for its warmth, friendliness, and genuine interest in spiritual things. They truly have an interest in Bible study. They will respond to a spiritual challenge. They take notes during class, they participate in the ProTeen quiz, and they memorize Scripture.

But the defining characteristic of this group is their closeness to each other. They are like family. They genuinely enjoy being together, whether it's playing or praying.

the fiery red youth group

This group is on fire for the Lord. They not only enjoy being with each other, but they also have a desire to serve the Lord with their lives. This group is committed to full-time Christian service, has a genuine burden for the Lord, and is bold in their Christian outreach. These teens are unusually mature in their faith.

the difference between the two groups

The basic difference between the warm yellow and fiery red groups is one of spiritual depth and maturity. Whereas the yellow group is interested in spiritual things, the red group has committed their lives to them. The red group does not just go out on soul winning activities; they are serious about it and are burdened to reach people for Christ. They are far bolder than the yellow group.

Both groups are a delight to have, but both are extremely rare!

how to work with the yellow and red youth groups

teach them to meditate

yellow and red groups are spiritually mature enough to learn the art of scriptural meditation. While this is often attempted at the lower levels with some degree of success, it is far more effective with the yellow and red teens.

Meditation is the most basic and perhaps most important Christian exercise (with the possible exception of prayer). In fact, meditation is the beginning and ending point for spiritual growth! If you want strong, godly teens, teach them to meditate.

However, meditation must be correctly understood. The New Age movement and many Far Eastern religions practice meditation. Why? Because Satan knows its power and has imitated it in false religions. Sadly, false prophets practice it far more than true believers. In fact, many Christians shy away from meditation because it is practiced so widely among cults. Proper biblical meditation, however, is taught in Scripture.

Biblical meditation must have a proper focus to be effective. It must focus in two areas: the Word of God and the works of God. Meditation must center on one subject—the Godhead. All other meditation is a waste. Thus, if you are to develop godly yellow and red teens, you must get them involved in meditation on God in the Word and in His providences (God's works).

Romans 12:1–2 tells us to do three things: (1) present our bodies, (2) practice non-conformity to the world, and (3) renew our minds. Of the three, only one promises to transform our lives—renewing the mind. Yet 90% of our preaching to teens emphasizes the first two things. Teens can come forward at every invitation and can separate totally from the world; but if they do not renew their minds, they will not be transformed. This point must not be missed! It is meditation that transforms lives.

Psalm 1:1–3 reminds us that the blessed man is the man who meditates in the law of God day and night. Joshua is promised great success for doing the same thing (Joshua 1:8). These and dozens of other passages remind us that it is through meditation on God in His Word and in His providences that we fall in love with the Lord. Yet we seldom teach this to our teens, and we almost never give them a program that actually develops their ability to meditate.

Thus, you must (1) teach them the importance of meditation and (2) provide them with the tools and programs necessary to assist their meditation.

Will meditation work with green and white youth groups? Absolutely! In fact, it is necessary for all believers at any level of spiritual development. We emphasize it with the yellow and red groups, however, because it is the one exercise that can keep them growing even when they reach this stage of spiritual development.

For further information on meditation, look at our study, *Mighty Through God*.

challenge them to growth through exposure

Yellow and red groups must be challenged to further growth by exposure in three areas.

good music

Teens struggle with music—even the solid, mature teens. What they need is an alternative. It is not enough to ask them to give up the world's music. They must have something to take its place. Thus, it is important that they see and hear solid musical groups (usually Christian college groups) and have the opportunity to purchase tapes and CDs of these groups.

A word of caution is in order. Don't feed their fleshly desires for music that appeals to the body but has little effect on the soul. Be careful of the groups and music to which they are exposed. A good rule of thumb is to make sure the music (not just the words) matches the character of God in the following ways.

God Is Orderly

Music that is characterized by constant clashing of sounds and chaotic rhythmic beats is a violation of God's character.

God Is Our Father

Make sure the words emphasize a father–son relationship, not a lover relationship. We are not His lover; we are His children. The sound of the music should not be dreamy or romantic. It must be in keeping with the majesty and greatness of a holy, awesome God.

God Is Absolute

The idea of relativism is foreign to God's nature. Everything He does is yea or nay—no in between. He admonishes us to let our "yea be yea" and our "nay be nay." Art reflects the philosophy of its designer. In an age of relativism, modern art gave us splotches of color that somehow represented a barn or landscape. Nothing was real; it was surreal. This is contrary to God. Thus, our music should not be characterized by slurring and sliding all over the keyboard.

God Is Holy

The music and the words must emphasize the holiness of our God, not the biological drives of our bodies.

christian colleges

Yellow and red youth groups are ripe for Christian colleges. They should be exposed to those your church supports through college trips, a college corner (a special table or shelf in the youth department stocked with the latest catalogs and brochures of the colleges you support), and visits to your church by college groups.

missions

Yellow and red groups should hear the challenge of good missionaries. Further, a missions trip should be planned at least every three years. You should also get them involved in reading missionary biographies.

provide them with leadership opportunities

Yellow and red teens are your leaders. They must have opportunities for exercising leadership or they will not continue to develop, and soon their fire will die. Many opportunities are available. A partial listing includes:

- Captain of youth group teams
- Officer of your youth group
- Leading rest home services
- Planning and conducting youth activities
- Preaching and serving opportunities in the church

- Making announcements
- Leading singing
- Leading prayer groups in youth meetings

All of these are important for the continued development of your teens. In particular, they should be given some responsibility in planning and conducting activities and taking an active leadership role in youth group meetings.

Why does the youth pastor have to make all the announcements? Let a teen make them.

Why does the youth pastor have to lead in prayer time? Let a teen ask for prayer requests and lead in prayer time. Let another teen give a three-minute devotional.

Have a different group of teens plan an activity and take care of running it. During the author's early years at Falls Road Baptist Church, he planned a yearly extravaganza. The teens themselves had to plan the program, handle promoting it, and build the sets. The first such extravaganza was called FRB Ranch. The teens built a corral in the church parking lot. They wired it for lights, brought in an old covered wagon, cooked beans in a huge iron pot on an open fire, fixed up the youth building to resemble a barn, and built a platform (western style) for the program. The teens put on the program (all approved by the youth pastor, of course), and one of them gave a challenge at the end. Nearly 300 people attended, and the youth group caught fire.

honor them

Several times we have emphasized the principle that you get what you honor. This must not be forgotten relative to yellow and red teens. Make sure they are seriously and honorably held in high esteem by the entire church. Special recognition for their accomplishments should be given.

start a preacher boys' class

As your youth mature in the Lord, your young men will start seriously considering the ministry. It is time to start a Preacher Boys' class. Begin by teaching a book such as *Walking With the Giants* by Warren Wiersbe. This is an excellent book to introduce your young men to the giants of the past. It will also whet their appetites for purchasing books written by and about these men.

The author taught such a class to senior high boys and made books by and about these "giants" available for purchase. From this the boys developed a love for reading and book collecting. A bookstore grew out of that practice. Some young men had as many as 300 books by the time they graduated from high school.

I was even able to teach an elementary Greek class to the guys. They learned the Greek alphabet, a beginning Greek vocabulary, and were able to use a lexicon and Greek New Testament and take a stab at translating. It thrilled them and set them on fire to go to Bible college.

They can also be taught how to (1) study the Word, (2) write and give their personal testimony, and (3) outline and preach expository sermons.

develop their talents

Although this can be done from the very beginning (blue and green youth will be interested too), it is especially meaningful to the yellow and red. As they learn to sing, play musical instruments, preach, teach, use audio visuals, and make public speeches, you should provide public opportunities for them to use their skills.

Using trained, godly teens does two things: (1) it provides them the opportunity for service, and (2) it honors them before the church. Both are necessary for the development of a godly youth group.

provide them with outreach opportunities

Teens need opportunities to give out, not just take in. They should have many practical Christian outreach opportunities. Over the years, the author has used many such tools to develop the leadership and sharpen the godliness of his teens.

blitz tour

Our teens took a tour across North Carolina, conducting blitzes in a different town each night. A blitz is held in an outdoor park or ball field. Permission is obtained from city officials in advance. On the appointed day the teens go into the neighborhood surrounding the park, handing out leaflets and inviting the teens and children to the blitz. An hour or so later the teens gather as many children and teens as possible on the ball field and begin playing games with them. After an hour of fun, the youth group then provides skits and music to settle everyone down, and then one of the teens gives a message and an invitation. The teens counsel anyone who comes forward.

As we traveled across the state, we had a different host church each evening provide an evening meal and have their youth participate with us. The names of all contacts were given to the host church for follow-up. Many souls were saved, our youth group had revival, and later our church experienced revival when the youth group returned with their testimonies.

CIT leadership camp

CIT stands for counselor-in-training. Leading youth camps offer such a program for the hot teens in your youth group. It is good to get several of your teens involved in such a program during the summer. It will do wonders to develop the character and leadership of your yellow and red teens.

witnessing

It almost goes without saying that all saved teens need to be involved in giving out the gospel. The problem is that most teens don't know how or are afraid. We use tools to assist our youth in this important Christian exercise.

prayer meetings

Nothing can fan the flames of spiritual growth in the hearts of maturing teens like prayer meetings in homes. Make sure that they are prayer meetings and don't degenerate into social times with ten minutes given over to prayer.

First, announce the prayer meeting and invite all teens. However, provide for no refreshments. Play no games. This is a prayer meeting, nothing else. Begin the meeting with a short devotion. Then encourage teens to share testimonies. Finally, take prayer requests. You may have to prime the pump at the beginning by suggesting several requests yourself.

Next, divide the guys and girls and let them go to separate places in the house to pray. After the prayer time is over, head them home.

Why limit their time to prayer and testimonies only? So that (1) it will not degenerate into a social or gossip time, and (2) only the godly teens will want to come. Remember, you do not want to develop an elitist mentality among the group. You don't want the ungodly to feel that you are leaving them out. Thus, you make it open to all teens. On the other hand, you don't want so many ungodly teens that little or no real praying gets done. Thus, you make the evening so spiritually hot that the insincere will excuse themselves from the meeting.

how ProTeens can help keep the fires burning in your warm yellow and fiery red teens

blue, green, and white Positive Action For Christ materials

Don't overlook the fact that godly teens still need the basic, elementary ingredients used with the youth groups of other spiritual colors. Further, not all of your teens will be yellow or red even in the hottest youth groups. In fact, if your group is doing its job, there will be many blue, green, and white teens present at each meeting. They will need these materials.

fish: for witnessing christians

The fourth book in the Christian Growth Series, *Fish* contains eight in-depth lessons to teach your youth how to witness. It is ideal for the yellow and red youth groups.

ProTeens delta force youth program

Delta Force is a special ProTeen program designed for senior high yellow and red teens. It is open to all teens, but it is designed to be so hot that only the yellow and red youth will want to come. It lasts nine months and encompasses three types of curricula each year: 15 weeks of pure Bible study, 7 weeks of leadership training, and 8 weeks of Christian living studies (e.g., how to meditate, how to pray, how to pursue holiness, and how to get burdened for missions).

Delta Force is designed to work in conjunction with Sigma so that you are meeting the needs of all your teens from the ice blue to the fiery red. Further information is available online.

ProTeens classic yellow-red youth programs

The yellow–red versions of ProTeens Classic are the full–blown program first used by the author with his teens over twenty years ago. In addition to a more demanding scoring system, the following elements meet the specific needs of yellow and red groups.

practical christian work assignments

This version of ProTeens Classic encourages outreach for your hot teens. Many suggestions are given, and the leader is encouraged to add others.

ProTeen awards banquet

The ProTeen Awards Banquet is the perfect opportunity to honor the right kind of teens. This is built into the Classic program from the blue to red versions.

international scoring competition (ISC)

International Scoring Competition is available only with ProTeens Classic yellow–red (and Delta Force). Those teens who desire to enter pay a small fee. Each month their scores are sent to us for verification and compilation. We then publish a list of the top scorers in the world. At the end of the year, we award the top scorer a free trip to Israel! Winners are announced at The Wilds Camp each summer at the conclusion of ProTeen Week, one of the most exciting weeks of the year for your teens.

daily devotions

Positive Action For Christ has several different types of daily devotionals for your teens. See our web site or catalog for more information.

bolts & nuts

For more information on what holds a solid youth ministry together, order our Bolts & Nuts tape or CD. This resource gives thirteen points of a biblical youth philosophy—the foundation for a God–honoring ministry that lasts.

For more information and to order your free Positive Action For Christ Youth Ministry Catalog:

Write
Positive Action For Christ
PO Box 1948 • Rocky Mount, NC 27802–1948

Call
800–688–3008

Fax
252–977–2181

Web
www.positiveaction.org